Clever COGZ

THE BOOK OF

CARS AND TRUCKS

By Neil Clark

QEB

Quarto is the authority on a wide range of topics.

Quarto educates, entertains and enriches the lives of our readers—enthusiasts and lovers of hands-on living.

www.quartoknows.com

Author: Neil Clark
Illustrator: Neil Clark
Consultant: Oliver Green
Editor: Harriet Stone
Designer: Sarah Chapman-Suire

© 2019 Quarto Publishing plc
This edition first published in 2019
by QEB Publishing,
an imprint of The Quarto Group.
6 Orchard Road, Suite 100,
Lake Forest, CA 92630
T: +1 949 380 7510 F: +1 949 380 7575
www.QuartoKnows.com

A CIP record for this book is available from
the Library of Congress.

ISBN 978 1 78603 630 8

Manufactured in Shenzhen, China PP032019

9 8 7 6 5 4 3 2 1

MIX
Paper from
responsible sources
FSC® C001701

CONTENTS

The Car	**4**	Racing Car	**14**
Wheels	**6**	Camper	**16**
Tires	**7**	Truck	**18**
Car Controls	**8**	Dump Truck	**20**
Engines	**10**	Fire Engine	**22**
Car Design	**12**	Quiz	**24**

Hello, I'm Clever Cogz!

Follow me and my sidekicks, Nutty and Bolt, to learn all about motor cars and big trucks.

The Car

Cars are everywhere! They are an amazing invention, with lots of parts all working at the same time.

Cogz has bought a new car. Let's take a closer look...

Every car has a **number plate**, so that it can be tracked back to its owner. This one belongs to Cogz!

hood

engine

battery

COGZ1

Wheels
Most cars have four wheels, but some only have three. Have you ever seen a three-wheeled car? Learn more about wheels on page 6.

Tires
Most cars have a spare tire in the trunk, in case one gets a puncture. Learn about tires on page 7.

Fuel
Most cars use gasoline or diesel to power them. Some new cars use electricity instead. In the future maybe all cars will run on electricity.

gasoline

trunk

Fumes
Waste fumes come out of the exhaust. They are bad for the environment.

fuel tank

exhaust

Ooh, smelly!

Car Controls
The steering wheel is joined to the wheels, so the driver can turn left and right. Learn more about controls on page 8.

Engine Power
The engine is an important part of a car. Explore under the hood with Nutty and Bolt on page 10.

Wheels

Wheels make it easy to transport heavy things from one place to another. Do you know why wheels are always round? If wheels were square or triangle-shaped they wouldn't be able to roll along the ground.

That's wheely clever!

to the engine

axle

tire

Working Together

Car wheels work in pairs. Two wheels are joined together by an axle. The engine turns the axle, which turns the wheels and makes the car move along.

Tires

Tires go on the outside of a wheel. They are full of air. Do you know why cars have tires? Without them, wheels would get damaged on hard roads and car rides would be very bumpy.

It's ok, Cogz! We've got a spare tire in the trunk.

Oh no, a puncture!

Groovy Tires

Tires are made of rubber because it's strong but flexible. The grooves in the tire stop the car from skidding on the road.

My trainers have grooves too. They stop me slipping over!

Car Controls

There are lots of things a driver needs to push, pull, and turn to get a car from one place to another.

Steering Wheel

Without a steering wheel, a car would only be able to go in a straight line. Cogz is using a steering wheel to control his car along winding roads. Lots of clever parts are working together to turn the wheels.

wahooo!

steering column

steering wheel

wheel

axle

Engineers are building cars that control themselves, so they don't need drivers at all!

Reverse gear is for going backward.

Gear Stick

Most cars have five gears. The 1st gear is used to set off and climb steep hills. The 5th gear is used when going very fast! ZooooOOM! Some cars are automatic, which means the vehicle will change gear by itself. How clever!

CONN13

1 3 5

2 4 R

Engines

The engine is the most mind-blowing part of a car. It uses fuel to create energy and make the car GO! This is like how the food you eat gives you energy to move.

Let's look at what happens inside an engine.

2) The **spark plug** lights the fuel, which makes a tiny explosion.

5) **Waste fumes** come out.

1) **Fuel** is pumped into the engine.

BANG!

3) The explosion pushes down the **piston**.

4) The piston turns the **axle**, which turns the wheels!

Super Speedy
Lots of explosions happen every minute inside the engine, to keep the wheels turning. BRUM! BRUM!

Car Design

Cars come in all shapes and sizes. Modern cars look different from older cars. We now know that smooth, curved shapes are more aerodynamic than square shapes. Cars with a smooth shape can zoom through the air more easily and use less fuel to go fast.

1920　**1950**

1980　**2015**

air flow

If something has an aerodynamic shape, it means that air can flow around it easily.

My paper airplane is aerodynamic!

Car Safety

Cars have lots of gadgets to help keep passengers safe. When you get into a car you must always put on a seatbelt. If you have an accident, a seatbelt will keep you in your seat.

Don't start the trip until you hear the belt CLICK!

CLICK!

Mirrors let the driver see what's behind the car.

If you have a crash, the airbag will inflate like a big pillow.

COGZ1

Turn signals flash to show which direction the car is turning.

Headlights allow the driver to see the road and be seen by other drivers when it's dark.

B

13

Racing Car

As soon as the car was invented, people wanted to see how fast they could go. The first car race was more than 120 years ago.

It looks like Nutty wants to have a race. She's jumped in the driving seat!

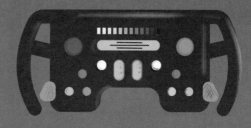

Steering Wheel
Some racing cars have a steering wheel that looks more like a computer game controller.

BRUM! BRUM!

The driver sits in the **cockpit**.

engine

8

Wings keep the car steady while traveling fast.

Racing drivers change their **tires** depending on the weather and the road.

Being a mechanic in the pit is very exciting.

Record breaker
The fastest car ever built was the Thrust Super Sonic. Its top speed was 763 miles per hour!
The Thrust Super Sonic was powered by jet engines, like a space rocket.

We're wearing ear protectors because it is very loud!

The car's **body** is made from lightweight material called carbon fiber.

A **pit-stop** is when a racing car stops during a race for more fuel, new tires, repairs, or to swap drivers.

Camper

A camper is like a home on wheels! You can drive a camper wherever you want to go. The furniture can be folded away when it's not being used.

Cogz met his friend Connie at the beach. She drove there in her camper.

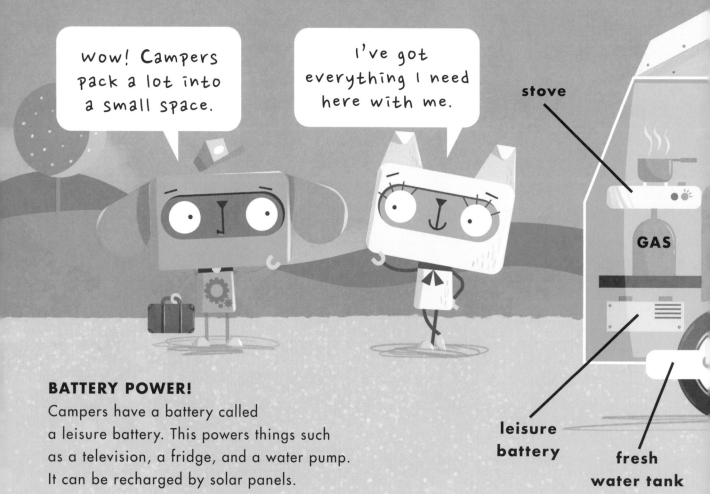

Wow! Campers pack a lot into a small space.

I've got everything I need here with me.

stove

GAS

leisure battery

fresh water tank

BATTERY POWER!
Campers have a battery called a leisure battery. This powers things such as a television, a fridge, and a water pump. It can be recharged by solar panels.

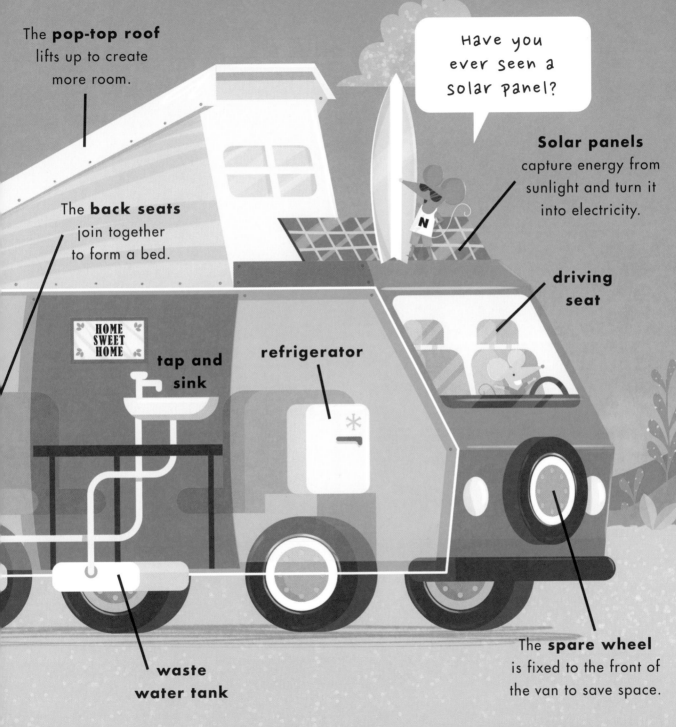

The **pop-top roof** lifts up to create more room.

The **back seats** join together to form a bed.

Have you ever seen a solar panel?

Solar panels capture energy from sunlight and turn it into electricity.

driving seat

HOME SWEET HOME

tap and sink

refrigerator

waste water tank

The **spare wheel** is fixed to the front of the van to save space.

Truck

We need trucks to move all kinds of cargo from one place to another. The clothes you're wearing probably traveled in a truck, and the food you ate for lunch...and this book you're reading!

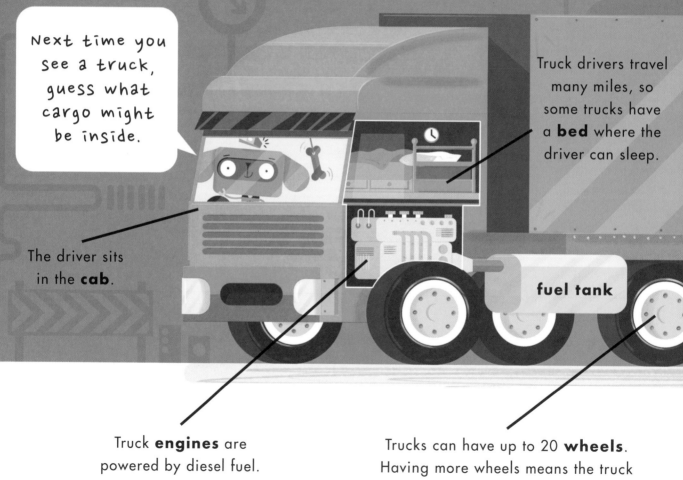

Next time you see a truck, guess what cargo might be inside.

Truck drivers travel many miles, so some trucks have a **bed** where the driver can sleep.

The driver sits in the **cab**.

fuel tank

Truck **engines** are powered by diesel fuel.

Trucks can have up to 20 **wheels**. Having more wheels means the truck can carry more weight.

Yum! Cheese!

The **cargo** goes in the **trailer**. Cargo means the items being transported.

You need to pass a test to drive a truck or a fork lift.

The sides of this trailer fold away, just like curtains. This makes it easy to load cargo on and off.

CHEESE

CHEESE

fuel tank

Fork lift
These clever machines have long, metal forks that can lift heavy loads.

forks

The **hydraulic lift** moves the forks up and down.

Levers control the forks.

Dump Truck

Dump trucks are used to transport large, heavy materials. They come in lots of different sizes! This is the world's biggest dump truck. It's called the BELAZ 75710.

It's so big that I can't see where Nutty and Bolt are hiding. Can you spot them?

tipper

Pistons push up the tipper to dump the load on the ground.

The driver sits in the **cab**.

Carrying rocks and coal is a dusty job. **Air filters** stop any dust from getting in the engine.

These diesel **engines** are four times more powerful than a family car.

COGZ1

Two **fuel tanks** hold 1,480 gallons of diesel. That's enough to fill 70 bath tubs!

wheels

The BELAZ 75710 carries coal and rocks and can hold over 490 tons—that's as heavy as 100 elephants!

Fire Engine

FIRE! FIRE! In an emergency, firefighters need a vehicle that will help them put a fire out. Fire engines are jam-packed with tools and equipment to help save the day.

Can you make a sound like a fire engine?

Ladders are used to reach tall buildings.

Foam is used to put out oil fires.

The **water tank** holds 400 gallons of water. That's 18 bath tubs full!

Two firefighters are needed
to hold a **hose** steady when
it's blasting out water.

Water or foam
is squirted from
the **water cannon**.

Yippee!

Nee-Naw,
Nee-Naw!

Warning lights allow
other drivers to see
a fire engine coming.

*FIRE is written
backward so that
other drivers can read
it in their mirrors.*

Reflectors are made
from a material that
glows in the dark.

The **siren** makes a very loud
noise so drivers know to
move out of the way.

We've come to the end of the road! What have you learned about cars and trucks?

Nutty and Bolt have come up with six questions. Let's see if we can answer them!

1. Most cars are powered by gasoline or diesel, but what else can a car run on?

2. How many gears does a car usually have?

3. Which is more aerodynamic, a square shape or a smooth shape?

4. What's the first thing you must do when you get into a car?

5. How much weight can the world's biggest dump truck carry?

6. What is the name of the fastest car ever built?

Answers
1. Electricity, 2. 5 gears, 3. A smooth shape, 4. Fasten your seatbelt, 5. 490 tons, 6. The Thrust Supersonic